Warm Little Knits

Classic Norwegian Two-Color Pattern Knitwear

Warm Little Knits

Classic Norwegian Two-Color Pattern Knitwear

Grete Letting

TS

TRAFALGAR SQUARE
North Pomfret, Vermont

First published in the United States of America in 2012 by
Trafalgar Square Books
North Pomfret, Vermont 05053

Originally published in Norway in 2002 by N.W. Damm & Søn AS
2nd edition, published in 2011

© 2002, 2011 Cappelen Damm AS
English translation © 2012 Trafalgar Square Books

ISBN: 978-1-57076-540-7

Library of Congress Control Number: 2011942247

Translation: Carol Huebscher Rhoades
Book Design: Charlotte Jørgensen
Photography: Anders Corneliussen, Tor Leiv Pedersen (page 26)
Pattern charts: Grete Letting

Printed in China

10 9 8 7 6 5 4 3 2 1

Contents

Preface

A while ago, in a Handcraft shop in Jølster, Norway, I saw a pair of socks that were similar to the pair I named Jenny. Since then I have knit small garments inspired by old mitten motifs. I think it is particularly fun to knit socks. Knitting socks all in two-color stranded knitting makes them not just pretty but very durable.

At the beginning it was difficult to get the pattern to work out well down the heel. Then I discovered how to shape the heel to suit the pattern. It was simply a matter of experimentation and practice.

I've found mitten patterns from all around Norway. I've bought old knitting books and weekly magazines from the 1940's in flea markets and I've looked at the many pairs of mittens my mother-in-law in Sogn and Fjordane has knitted in the course of her long life. Whenever I meet anyone with fine mittens, I borrow them, chart the pattern, and knit socks.

I've thought about writing this book for a long time. I would like to thank the basic education department at Damm (and Inger Landsem's father who knit a scarf with the eight-pointed star on it) for their persistent encouragement.

I knit all the garments and patterns in this book except for the hat and socks for Gunn. Gunn Grøndal knit the hat with the checkerboard jacket shown in the photo on page 26, and she knit the socks especially for this book. I received help from the hobby book editor at Damm and yarn from SGS Textiles and Hobby Inc. and am very appreciative of their support.

I would also like to thank the volunteer photo models, Kine, Eivind, Petter, Liv, Marthe, Birgit, and Lars. Thanks also to Asker Museum who let us use the house and grounds for the photo sessions and to the photographer, Anders, for the lovely pictures.

Oslo, Norway, September 2002
Grete Letting

Gauge and Pattern Knitting

On the ball band, yarn companies show a suggested needle size that you ought to use to knit the garment the correct size. For many knitters, this suggestion doesn't correspond to how they actually knit (at least in my case). I almost always use needles one U.S. / one half metric size smaller than those recommended on the ball band because I knit more loosely than "normal". Some patterns are easy to decrease at the sides and I do this when I want a smaller garment than the one described in the pattern. Other knitters knit more tightly than the recommended gauge, so they should use one U.S. / one half metric or larger size needle. Check your gauge before you knit!

Yarn tension

When you are knitting a two-color stranded knitting pattern, be sure the pattern strands don't hang loosely on the wrong side, you should twist them around each other as you knit. As a rule, most good knitting patterns suggest that you knit no more than five stitches between color twists or catches. In principle you shouldn't knit more than five stitches before you catch the other color with the working strand. However, I prefer to find a place where the color I am knitting is knit on the previous row and twist the colors at that point. That way the other color is not visible on the right side. Sometimes you might have to twist the yarns, for example, a red strand in the middle of a blue area. It is important to make sure that the stitch you are knitting is the same tension as the other, and that it doesn't make a loop on the back. Be careful when doing this so the red strand won't show through the blue.

How to Knit a Sock

Ribbing

Of course you can knit the ribbing as long as you want. The ribbed cuffs are short on almost all the socks in this book because there is patterning instead.

Toe shaping

On the patterned socks, the toe is pointed because otherwise the pattern would be broken.

In the photos below you can see that there are patterned areas on each side of a gray stitch. The red stitch on the right side of the gray stitch is decreased by knitting two stitches together with red yarn. The gray stitch is always knit. Slip the next stitch knitwise, knit 1 stitch with red and pass the slipped stitch over. All of the socks in this book have the same toe shaping.

Heel

On two of the three types of heel shaping I have used, you knit a heel flap using two of the four needles. I have numbered these two needles as needle 1 and needle 4. The length of the heel flap depends on the size of the sock.
After the heel flap is completed, you work the heel gusset.
Slipping sts on heel gussets: When slipping sts at beginning of rows on heel gussets, always slip purlwise with yarn held to WS.

Shaping the Heel/Heel Gusset

Heel with a smooth decrease line

When you shape the heel as for the sock for Yvonne on p. 13, you need a heel with a smooth, even decrease line. It is easy to follow the pattern when you decrease this way.

A Heel that makes it easy to follow the pattern

You'll find this heel on the socks for Andris on p. 51. It is the same pattern as on the inside of the ball band for some of the sock yarns such as Ragge yarn from Gjestal.

Heel without decreases

You'll find this heel on Håvard on p. 65. It is worked back and forth with increasingly more stitches on each row so it becomes higher at the center.

After the shaping for these three heels, you pick up and knit stitches along each side of the heel flap and decrease the extra stitches for a gusset as described in the pattern instructions. The smoothest way to pick up the stitches is with a crochet hook. To add in both pattern colors, alternate the colors as you pick up and knit.

Heel shaped like a toe

On the socks for Jorun on p. 43, you knit in a strand of waste yarn where the heel should be. The rest of the sock is knitted before you begin the heel. It is the easiest way to work in pattern on the heel but these socks do not have the best fit. This heel is best for "night socks" or "cabin socks" instead of slippers.

Foot Gussets

When picking up and knitting stitches along each side of the heel flap, make sure that you pick up the same number of stitches on each side unless otherwise specified. Each pattern indicates a suggested number of stitches to pick up but you may need to pick one or two more or less depending on the length of the heel flap. Too many stitches, though, and the heel will pucker; too few and it will pull in too tightly. Many of the patterns in this book decrease on alternate rounds for a better fit. Experiment and see what works best for you.

Shoe Sizes and Foot Lengths

Measure the foot length as follows:

1. Put a piece of paper on the floor with one short end at a wall.
2. Put your foot on the paper with your heel against the wall.
3. Draw a line on the paper at the top of your big toe.
4. Measure the distance from the edge of the paper to the toe line.

Shoe Sizes (U.S. / Metric)	Foot Length (in / cm)
Child's 5 / 20	4.5-4.7 / 11.4-12
Child's 6 / 21	4.7-5 / 12-12.7
Child's 6 / 22	5-5.3 / 12.7-13.5
Child's 7 / 23	5.3-5.6 / 13.5-14.1
Child's 8 / 24	5.6-5.8 / 14.1-14.7
Child's 8 ½ /25	5.8-6 / 14.7-15.3
Girl's 8 ½ / 26	6-6.3 / 15.3-16
Girl's 9 ½ / 27	6.3-6.5 / 16-16.6
Girl's 10 ½ / 28	6.5-6.8 / 16.6-17.3
Girl's 11 ½ / 29	6.8-7.1 / 17.3-18
Girl's 12 / 30	7.1-7.4 / 18-18.7
Girl's 13 / 31	7.4-7.6 / 18.7-19.3
Girl's 1 / 32	7.6-7.9 / 19.3-20
Girl's 1 ½ / 33	7.9-8.1 / 20-20.7
Women's 4 ½ / 34	8.1-8.4 / 20.7-21.3
Women's 5 / 35	8.4-8.6 / 21.3-21.9
Women's 6 / 36	8.6-8.9 / 21.9-22.6
Women's 7 / 37	8.9-9.2 / 22.6-23.3
Women's 8 / 38	9.3-9.4 / 23.3-23.9
Women's 9 / 39	9.4-9.7 / 23.9-24.6
Women's 10 / 40	9.7-10 / 24.6-25.3
Women's 11 / 41	10-10.2 / 25.3-26
Women's 12, Men's 8 / 42	10.2-10.5 / 26-26.7
Men's 9 / 43	10.5-10.7 / 26.7-27.3
Men's 10 ½ / 44	10.7-11.2 / 27.3-28.4
Men's 11 ½ / 45	11.2-11.5 / 28.4-29.1
Men's 13 / 46	11.5-11.8 / 29.1-29.9

Abbreviations

BO	bind off (British: cast off)
CC	contrast color
cm	centimeter(s)
CO	cast on
dpn	double-pointed needles
g	gram(s)
in	inch(es)
k	knit

k1fb	knit into front and then back of same stitch
k2tog	knit 2 sts together
M1	make 1: lift strand between 2 sts and knit into back loop
MC	main color
mm	millimeter(s)
p	purl
p2tog	purl two stitches together
psso	pass slipped stitch over

rem	remain(ing)
rnd(s)	round(s)
RS	right side
sl	slip
ssk	(slip 1 knitwise) 2 times, knit the sts together through back loops (can substitute for sl 1, k1, psso)
st(s)	stitch(es)
tbl	through back loop

Eivind

SOCKS, SCARF, AND HAT

Size: 6 months – 1 year
Yarn: Shown here: Gjestal Baby 8/4 cotton
(100% mercerized cotton, 187 yd [171 m], 50 g)
4-ply Fingering
Yarn amounts for the set:
100 g white 801
100 g orange 823
50 g green 817
Needles: U.S. sizes 1.5-2.5 / 2.5-3 mm--set of 5
dpn for socks/scarf and a short circular for hat
Gauge: 27-28 sts = 4 in / 10 cm
Adjust needle sizes to obtain correct gauge if
necessary.
Pattern repeat is a multiple of 12 + 1 sts

Socks

50 g white 801
50 g green 817
50 g orange 823

The pattern charts are on page 10.

With white and 2 dpn U.S. 1.5 / 2.5 mm, CO 48 sts. Knit 3 rows back and forth (2 ridges). Divide sts over 4 dpn and join. Work the cuff pattern in stockinette. Purl 1 round for the foldline and then work 4 rnds in stockinette with MC (white). Turn the knitting inside out. Knit 3 rnds stockinette and then begin the leg pattern. If necessary for correct gauge, change to larger needle size. When piece measures approx. 3 ¼ in / 8 cm from the foldline, work the heel flap.

Heel flap

Place 24 sts onto one dpn and work the heel pattern back and forth for approx. 1 in / 2.5 cm following the chart. Next, shape heel gusset.

Heel Gusset

Begin with RS facing. Make sure that you pick up both colors when you continue with the heel pattern and make sure that the motifs match. Knit 16 sts, slip the next st, knit the next st and psso. Turn. Sl 1 and tighten yarn slightly. Purl until 8 sts remain on the needle, p2tog. Turn. K9, sl 1, k1, psso; turn. Continue the same way, with one st more before the decrease, until all the sts have been worked. Divide the sts over 2 needles.

Knit the sts beginning at the center of the heel (sts on ndl 1). Pick up and knit approx. 8 sts along the edge using a crochet hook if necessary. Knit the sts on the next 2 needles (needles 2 and 3)

in main pattern. Pick up and knit sts on the other side of the heel flap with the crochet hook, and place them with the sts on ndl 4. The round begins at the center of the heel under the foot.

Continue around in the main pattern over all the sts. Decrease at the end of ndl 1 with k2tog. Decrease at the beginning of ndl 4 with sl 1, k1, psso. Decrease the same way on every round until 48 sts remain. Continue around in main pattern until the foot is approx. 3 ¼ in / 8 cm from back of heel or desired length.

Toe Shaping

Knit sts on ndl 1 until 3 sts remain. K2tog with green. Knit the last st with white. At beginning of ndl 2, slip 1, k1 with green and psso. Knit the remaining sts on needle. Knit across ndl 3 until 3 sts remain and decrease as for ndl 1; decrease on ndl 4 as for ndl 2. Decrease the same way on every round until 6 sts remain. Cut yarn and pull through remaining sts. Weave in all ends neatly on WS. Fold the cuff along the foldline. Knit the other sock the same way. Steam press socks gently to block.

Scarf

50 g orange 823
50 g white 801
50 g green 817 (the green can be leftover yarn from the socks/hat)

With MC and needles U.S. 1.5 or 2.5 / 2.5 or 3 mm, CO 50 sts; join, being careful not to twist cast-on row. Knit 3 rnds with white. Work 1 pattern repeat with green as CC and then change the CC

to orange. See chart for the scarf. If you don't want to change the contrast colors as shown here, you can make the scarf the same on both sides. Make the scarf as long as you like. Finish with a green pattern repeat and 3 rnds white. BO. This scarf is approx. 31 ½ in / 80 cm long.

Hat

50 g white 801
50 g green 817
50 g orange 823 (the pattern colors can be leftover yarn from the scarf/socks)

With short circular U.S. 1.5 / 2.5 mm and MC, CO 120 sts. Knit 3 rows back and forth (2 ridges) and then join to work pattern border in the round to the foldline on the hat (begin at the top of the chart and work down). Purl 1 rnd on RS for the foldline and then continue with 4 rnds stockinette. Turn work inside out so the RS is on the other side. Knit 2 rnds stockinette, and then work in basic pattern (see basic pattern for the socks) until hat is 7 in / 18 cm from foldline. Complete a pattern repeat before shaping if possible. Cut green yarn.

Top Shaping
(K2, k2tog) around.
Knit 1 rnd.
(K2, k2tog) around. Cut yarn and pull through rem sts, pulling top together.

Scarf and Hat

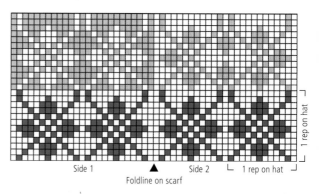

Side 1   ▲   Side 2   └ 1 rep on hat ┘

Foldline on scarf

1 rep on hat

Socks

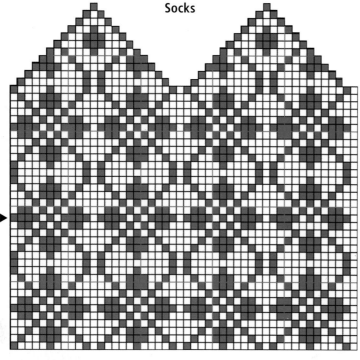

 Knit the heel here before you continue in pattern as described in the instructions.

Folded Brim

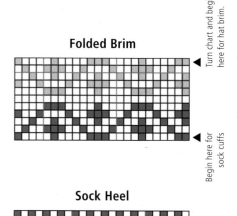

◄ Turn chart and begin here for hat brim.

◄ Begin here for sock cuffs

Sock Heel

Work back and forth in pattern

Yvonne

SOCKS, SCARF, AND HAT WITH TWO POMPOMS

Size: Women's medium, shoe sizes U.S. 6-7 / European 36-37

Yarn: Shown here: Gjestal Silja sock yarn (80% wool / 20% nylon, 164 yd [150 m], 50 g)

Light Sport / Heavy Fingering

Yarn amounts:

Socks: 100 g green 362 and 100 g rust red 363

Scarf: 150 g green 362 and 100 g rust red 363

Hat: 100 g green 362 and 50 g rust red 363

Needles: U.S. sizes 2.5 and 4 / 3 and 3.5 mm--set of 5 dpn for socks and short circulars for hat and scarf

Gauge: 26 sts = 4 in / 10 cm

Adjust needle sizes to obtain correct gauge if necessary.

If you knit the socks on needles U.S. 2.5 / 3 mm, they will be for shoe size U.S. 5 / Euro 35. If you use needles U.S. 4 / 3.5 mm, they will fit U.S. 6-7 / Euro 36-37.

With MC (rust red), CO 54 sts and divide onto 4 dpn; join, being careful not to twist cast-on row. Work 7 rnds k1tbl, p1 rib. Knit 1 rnd, increasing 8 sts evenly spaced around to 62 sts. Work charted sock pattern (see next page) until piece measures 5 ¼ in / 13 cm.

Heel Flap

Put the 29 sts of ndls 1 and 4 together on 1 needle. Work back and forth in pattern for approx. 1 ½ in / 4 cm. Place marker around center st.

Heel Gusset

Begin with RS facing you. Follow the pattern as well as possible as you shape the gusset. Work past the center st until 9 sts rem, sl 1, k1, psso; turn. Sl 1 purlwise and tighten yarn slightly. Purl across in pattern until 9 sts rem. P2tog tbl (insert needle in first st and then the second st from the RS and purl them together). This decrease is mirror image of the decrease on the other side of the gusset. After you've completed the shaping, these decreases will form a line along the heel.

Turn. Sl 1 and tighten yarn. Knit in pattern until 8 sts rem, k2tog and turn. Sl 1 and tighten yarn. Work until 8 sts rem and p2tog tbl; turn. Continue the same way until all the sts have been worked.

With ndl 4, knit to and including the center st. Knit the rem sts on ndl 1. Pick up and knit about 12 sts along the heel flap using a crochet hook. To maintain the color sequence, alternate the two colors when picking up. Make sure the last st is MC (rust). Work across ndls 2 and 3 in the bird motif. Beginning with MC (rust), pick up and knit about 12 sts along the other edge of heel flap with the crochet hook. Place these sts on ndl 4 and work to center st.

Now you can shape the foot gussets (there are 14 sts on ndl 1 and 15 sts on ndl 4). Work across ndl 1 until 2 sts rem and knit 2 together with rust. Work across ndls 2 and 3 in pattern. Begin ndl 4 with sl 1, k1 with rust and psso, complete rnd. Decrease the same way on every round until 62 sts rem. Continue in pattern until foot is desired length.

Toe Shaping

While shaping toe, continue the pattern on the sole. On the instep, finish as shown on the chart. Begin decreasing on ndl 4: Sl 1, k1 with rust, psso, knit across ndl. Ndl 1: Knit across until 2 sts rem, k2tog with rust. On the next ndl (2), k1, sl 1 rust, k1 with rust, psso. Work across ndl 3 until 3 sts rem, k2tog with rust and k1. Continue decreasing the same way on every round until 6 sts remain. Cut yarn and pull through remaining sts; tighten. Weave in all ends neatly on WS.

Make the other sock the same way.

With MC and U.S. 2.5 / 3 mm circular, CO 70 sts; join,

Socks

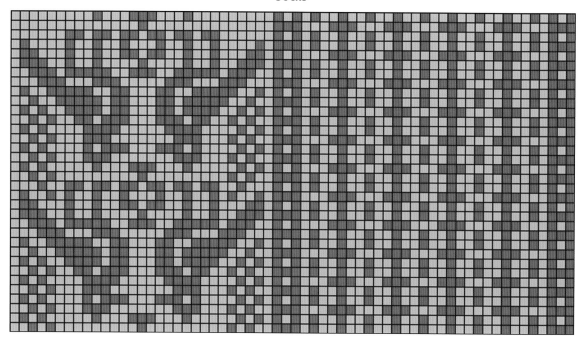

Toe Shaping for Instep of Sock

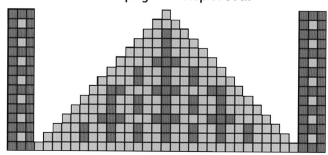

Hat and Scarf

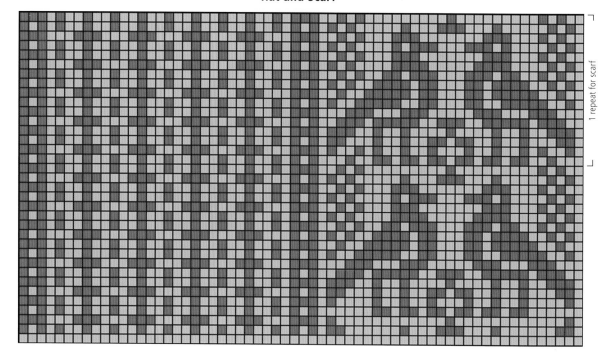

1 repeat for scarf

being careful not to twist cast-on row. Work 7 rnds k1tbl, p1 rib as for socks. Change to US 4 / 3.5 mm circular and work in pattern following the chart. The scarf shown is approx. 49 ¼ in / 125 cm long, but, of course, you can make yours as long as you like. When you are at the halfway point, reverse the chart to work the birds top down as on the socks. Finish with 7 rnds k1tbl, p1 on smaller needles and then BO. Gently steam press the scarf and then sew the ends together neatly. If you want, you can add fringe or pompoms to the ends.

With MC and U.S. 2.5 / 3 mm circular, CO 132 sts; join, being careful not to twist cast-on row. Work 7 rnds k1tbl, p1 rib as for scarf. Change to U.S. 4 / 3.5 mm circular and work in pattern following the chart until hat is approx. 7 ½ in 19 cm long. Knit 5 rnds with MC and then turn hat inside out. Begin binding off where you see an arrow pointing towards the pattern. Join the sets of sts with three-needle bind-off. Hold needles parallel (RS faces RS). Using a third needle, insert it through first st on each needle and knit together, *knit each first st on left needles together and then pass st on right needle over to bind off; rep from * until all sts have been bound off. Weave in all ends neatly on WS. Gently steam press hat. Make pompoms and sew securely to each top corner.

Tormod

Socks

With smaller dpn and black, CO 52 sts; divide over 4 dpn and join, being careful not to twist cast-on row. Work in striped k2, p2 rib as follows: 14 rnds black, 2 rnds red, 4 rnds black, 1 rnd red, 1 rnd black, 1 rnd red, 1 rnd black, 1 rnd red, 4 rnds black, 2 rnds red, 14 rnds black. Change to larger dpn and work 1 rnd with black, increase 8 sts evenly spaced around to 60 sts. Knit 2 rnds with red and then work the heel in charted pattern: Put 27 sts onto one needle and work back and forth in small diamond pattern (used for palm of mitten) until heel flap is approx. 2 1/2 in / 6 cm long.

Heel Gusset

Mark the center st of heel flap. Begin shaping on the RS, keeping pattern aligned as much as possible. Knit 5 sts past the center st, k2tog tbl, k1, and turn. Sl 1 purlwise and tighten yarn slightly. Purl (in pattern) to 3 sts past center st, p2tog, p1, turn. Sl 1, pulling yarn to tighten, k9, k2tog tbl, k1, turn. Sl 1, tighten yarn, p10, p2tog, p1, turn. Continue decreasing the same way until all the sts have been worked.

Foot Gussets

Ndl 1 begins at the center st. Pick up and knit about 12 sts along the heel flap using the crochet hook. Alternate the two colors as you pick up sts, making sure that the last st is red. Work across ndls 2 and 3 in star pattern. Pick up about 12 sts along other side of heel flap using crochet hook. The

SOCKS AND MITTENS

Size: Men's medium, shoe size U.S. Men's 8 / European 42
Yarn: Shown here: Gjestal Vestland yarn
(100% wool, 109 yd [100 m], 50 g)
4-ply Worsted
Yarn amounts:
Socks: 150 g black 201 and 100 g rust red 209
Mittens: 150 g black 201 and 100 g rust red 209
Needles: U.S. sizes 4 and 6 / 3.5 and 4 mm--set of 5 dpn
Gauge: 23 sts = 4 in / 10 cm
Adjust needle sizes to obtain correct gauge if necessary.

first st should be red. Knit sts on ndl 1 until 2 sts rem and k2tog with red. Knit in star pattern across ndls 2 and 3. Begin ndl 4 with red: sl 1, k1 with red, psso; finish rnd. Decrease the same way on every rnd until 60 sts remain. Continue in pattern on foot to desired length (on this sock, it is 6 1/4 in / 16 cm from the gusset).

Toe Shaping

Knit sts of ndl 1 until 2 st rem and k2tog with red. Begin ndl 2 with red or black to fit into pattern, sl the red st, knit next st with red and psso. Work across ndl 3 until 3 sts rem and k2tog with red; knit the last st with red or black depending on what fits into pattern. Begin ndl 4 with sl 1, knit next st with red, psso. Finish rnd. Decrease the same way on every rnd until 6 sts remain. Cut yarn and pull through rem sts; tighten. Weave in all ends neatly on WS and gently steam press sock to block.

Make the other sock the same way.

Mittens

With red yarn and smaller dpn, CO 52 sts; divide over 4 dpn and join, being careful not to twist cast-on row. Work in striped k2, p2 rib as follows: 3 rnds red, 4 rnds black, 1 rnd red, 1 rnd black, 1 rnd red, 1 rnd black, 1 rnd red, 4 rnds black, 2 rnds red, 4 rnds black.

Change to larger dpn and work following the chart. Work thumb gusset at point indicated on main chart. Increase with M1. Place the 13 thumb sts on a holder and then CO 10 over the gap = 60 sts total. Continue,

following the chart, decreasing for the mitten top as for the toe shaping on the socks.

Thumb

Divide the 13 sts onto 2 dpn and then pick up and knit 11 sts. Knit thumb following the thumb chart.

Make the other mitten the same way, reversing placement of thumb gusset on palm.

Socks and Mittens

Thumb

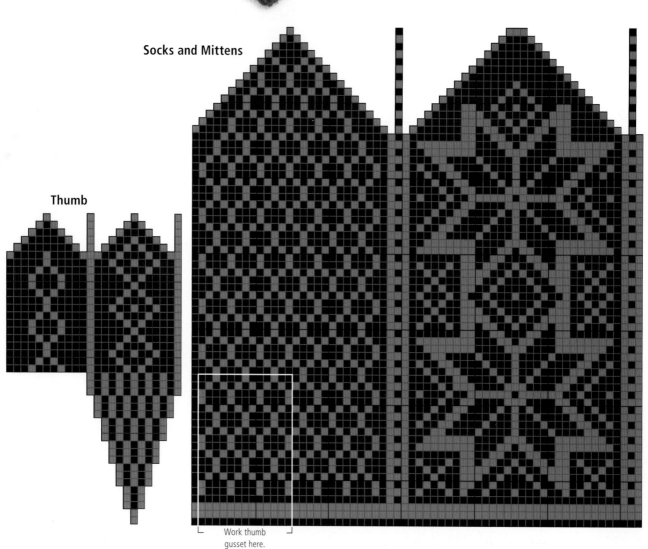

Work thumb gusset here.

Rigmor

SOCKS AND HEADBAND

Size: Women's medium, shoe size approx. U.S. 8 /
European 38

Yarn: Shown here: Gjestal Vestland yarn
(100% wool, 109 yd [100 m], 50 g)

4-ply Worsted

Yarn amounts:

Socks: 150 g gray 254 and 100 g red 240

Headband: yarn leftover from socks

Needles: U.S. sizes 2.5-4 / 3-3.5 mm--set of 5 dpn for socks
and short circular for headband

Gauge: 26 sts = 4 in / 10 cm

Adjust needle sizes to obtain correct gauge if necessary.

Socks

Headband

Socks

With smaller dpn and gray, CO 60 sts; divide over 4 dpn and join, being careful not to twist cast-on row. Work 7 rnds in k1tbl, p1 rib. Knit 1 rnd, increasing 6 sts evenly spaced around (66 sts total). Work in pattern following the chart until sock leg is approx. 6 ¼ in / 16 cm long.

Heel

Place the 30 sts for heel onto 1 ndl and work 12 rows back and forth in pattern. Begin shaping on RS. Place a marker between sts 15 and 16. Knit 4 sts past marker, k2tog, k1; turn. Sl 1 and tighten yarn. Purl until 4 sts past marker (keeping pattern aligned), p2tog, p1; turn. Knit until you come to the st you slipped, knit it and the next st tog, k1, turn. Continue the same way until you have worked all the sts. Needle 1 now begins at the center st. Knit sts on ndl 1. Pick up and knit 13-14 sts along side of heel flap using crochet hook, alternating red and gray. Knit across ndls 2-3 in pattern. Pick up and knit 13-14 sts on ndl 4 using crochet hook and alternating red and gray. Make sure that the pattern is aligned when you begin next rnd on ndl 1.

Foot Gussets

Use the red st nearest the foot to decrease. Knit until 1 st before the red st on ndl 1 and knit it tog with red yarn. Sl the red st on ndl 4, knit next st with red and psso. Decrease the same way on every rnd until 66 sts remain. Continue in pattern until foot is 6 in / 15 cm from the gusset or to desired length.

Toe Shaping

Use red for all decreases. Ndl 1: Knit until 2 sts rem and then knit the red st together with the st before it on ndl 1. On ndl 2, knit the gray st, sl 1 red, knit the next st with red and psso. Knit rem sts on ndl. Ndl 3: work as for ndl 1 and ndl 4 as for ndl 2. Decrease the same way until 6 sts remain. Cut yarn and pull end through rem sts; pull tight. Weave in all ends neatly on WS. Gently steam press sock to block.
Make the other sock the same way.

Headband

The pattern motif is a multiple of 16. With short circular U.S. 2.5 / 3 mm and red, CO 128 sts; join, being careful not to twist cast-on row. Knit 8 rnds. Change to gray and work eyelet rnd: *k2tog, yo*; rep * to * around. Continue in pattern following the chart. After charted rows, work another eyelet rnd with gray and then knit 8 rnds with red. BO. Gently steam press headband, folding facings in at each eyelet row. Seam cast-on and bind-off rows together with mattress st on RS.

Bente

Socks

With smaller dpn and gray, CO 60 sts; divide over 4 dpn and join, being careful not to twist cast-on row. Work 3 rnds in k1tbl, p1 rib. Work in 2-color rib for approx. 1 ¼ in / 3 cm with white over the knit sts and gray over the purls. Make sure stitches don't draw in too much. Knit 1 rnd gray and then work 3 rnds k1tbl. P1 rib, increasing 8 sts evenly spaced around the last round (68 sts total). Change to larger needles and work in pattern following the chart. Set up pattern, dividing the sts onto dpn as follows:

Ndl 1: K1tbl with white, p1 gray, 15 sts pattern (the first pattern st is knit with gray throughout).

SOCKS, HEADBAND, AND WRIST WARMERS

Size: Women's medium, shoe sizes approx. U.S. 6-7 / European 36-37
Yarn: Shown here: Gjestal Silja sock yarn (80% wool / 20% nylon, 164 yd [150 m], 50 g) Light Sport / Heavy Fingering
Yarn amounts:
Set: 150 g gray 330 and 100 g white 300
Needles: U.S. sizes 2.5 and 4 / 3 and 3.5 mm--set of 5 dpn for socks and wrist warmers; short circular for headband
Gauge: 26 sts = 4 in / 10 cm
Adjust needle sizes to obtain correct gauge if necessary.

later on. Continue in pattern until you have worked another 4 ¾ in / 12 cm (or to desired length of foot to toe shaping).

Toe Shaping

Decreases are worked along the gray knit sts throughout. *On ndl 1, sl the gray st, knit next st with gray and psso. Continue in pattern to end of ndl. On ndl 2, knit in pattern to 1 st before the gray st; k2tog with gray yarn. Rep from * over ndls 3 and 4.

Decrease as set on every rnd until 12 sts remain. Cut yarn and pull through rem sts, tighten.

Heel Shaping – as for the Toe

Pick up 34 sts above and below the waste yarn and remove waste yarn using tip of a knitting needle. Knit 1 rnd following the pattern on the heel chart. The sts you have picked up should follow the pattern with twisted knit sts and purl sts as on the heel. On the side that continues the back of the sock, it is easy to follow the sock pattern. Under the foot you can finish with stripes as shown on the heel chart.

Cut yarn and pull end through rem sts; tighten. Weave in ends neatly on WS and gently steam press sock to block.
Make the other sock the same way.

Headband

Use leftover yarns from socks or
50 g gray 330
50 g white 300

Ndl 2: 14 sts pattern (the last st of pattern should be knit with gray throughout), p1 gray, k1tbl, p1 gray.
Ndl 3: Work as for ndl 1.
Ndl 4: Work as for ndl 2.
Continue in charted pattern until leg measures 6 in / 15 cm. Knit sts on ndls 2 and 3 on waste yarn. You will knit the heel over these sts

With smaller size short circular and MC (gray), CO 132 sts; join, being careful not to twist cast-on row.
Knit 8 rnds and then work 3 rnds k1tbl, p1 rib. Decide if you need to change to larger size

Socks

circular for the two-color rib (we didn't on the model shown). Make sure that the two-color rib doesn't draw in too much. Work 15 rnds k1tbl with white, p1 with gray. Work 3 rnds with gray only in k1 tbl, p1 rib and then knit 8 rnds with gray. BO. Cut yarn and weave in ends neatly on WS. Gently steam press to block letting top and bottom edges roll (don't press them too hard).

Wrist Warmers

Work as for headband, casting on 48 or 50 sts depending on the fit you want.

● K1 tbl with white

☐ Purl 1 with gray

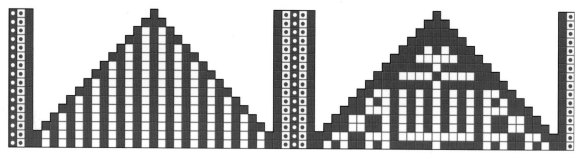

3-color Twisted Braid

Cast on all the sts for the garment onto one needle. Work the three colors in sequence. For each stitch, bring the backmost strand from below around the CO row and purl tbl (it is the easiest way to work). The strands will lie diagonally and make a decorative band.

Socks

With black and one needle, CO 62 sts. Work twisted braid with all three colors (see above). Divide the sts onto 4 dpn (onto size necessary for gauge) and work in charted pattern. On the Socks for Gunn, all the vertical black sts are purled for a "purl panel" and on the top of the foot (right side of the chart).

Gunn

CHECKED SOCKS AND HAT

Size: Women's medium, shoe size U.S. 8 / European 38

Yarn: Shown here: Gjestal Vestland yarn

(100% wool, 109 yd [100 m], 50 g)

4-ply Worsted

Yarn amounts:

100 g black 201

100 g purple 202

50 g green 256

Needles: U.S. sizes 4 and 6 / 3.5 and 4 mm--set of 5 dpn

for socks and short circular for hat

Gauge: 23 sts = 4 in / 10 cm

Adjust needle sizes to obtain correct gauge if necessary.

Heel

Place 32 sts on one needle and continue in pattern, working back and forth. After completing the heel flap, shape the gusset for the heel (this is not shown on the chart, so please read the following instructions).

Work with purple and black throughout. After 4 rnds with purple, make a black stripe. Gunn has worked the black stripes back and forth to save having to weave in ends. Begin shaping on RS. K23, sl 1, knit next st with black and psso. Turn. Purl 14 (don't forget to follow the pattern), purl the next 2 sts

tog tbl; turn. Knit 14 sts, decrease, and continue as set until you have worked all the sts on both sides. Divide the sts over 2 dpn again. Pick up and knit approx. 14 sts along the left side of the heel flap using a crochet hook, place these sts together with the sts on the left side of the heel. These sts are now on ndl 1. Work sts on ndls 2 and 3 following chart. Pick up approx. 14 sts along the right side of the heel flap with the crochet hook and place these sts together with sts from the right side of the heel onto ndl 4. Shape foot gussets:

Gunn Grøndal designed this hat and sock set to go with her checked jacket.

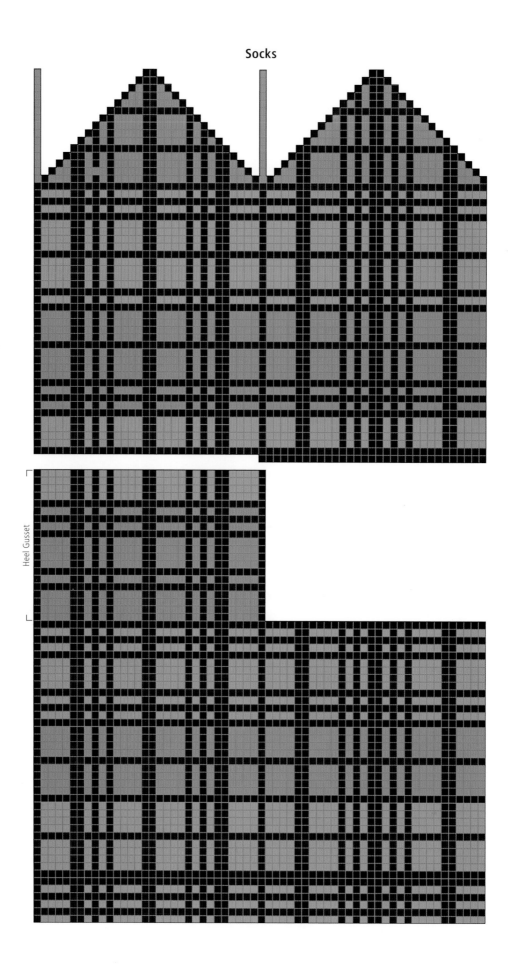

Heel Gusset

Work across ndl 1 until 2 sts rem and k2tog. Work sts of ndls 2 and 3 following chart. Begin ndl 4 with sl 1, k1 with black, psso. Work to end of round following chart. Continue to decrease the same way until 62 sts remain.

Toe Shaping
Work across ndl 1 to last 2 sts and end k2tog with black. Begin ndl 2 with k1 green. Sl 1, k1 with black, psso, work to end of ndl. Work across ndl 3 until 3 sts remain, k2tog with black, k1 with green. Begin ndl 4 with sl 1, k1 with black, psso, work to end of ndl.
Decrease the same way on every rnd until 6 sts remain. Cut yarn and pull end through rem sts; tighten. Weave in ends neatly on WS and gently steam press sock to block. Make the other sock the same way.

Hat

With black, CO 120 sts and work twisted braid (see above). Join to work in the round and work the hat following the chart. The charted repeat is 30 sts which is repeated 4 times.

Shaping (continue in charted pattern).
Where there are 4 same-color sts in a square, k2, k2tog.
Work 1 rnd without decreasing.
Where there are 2 purple sts – k2tog with the 2 purple sts.
Work 1 rnd without decreasing but following color pattern.
Knit 1 rnd with black.
Work the black/purple rnd once more.
Knit with black, working k2, k2tog.
Work 1 rnd with 1 black, 1 purple.
Knit 1 rnd black.
Knit 1 black, k1 green around.
With black, k2, k2tog so that the green st lies on top of decrease.
Next rnd with purple: k2, k2tog so the black st lies on top.
Next rnd with black: k2, k2tog with the purple st lying on top.
Continue with black only, decreasing until 5 sts remain.
Place these sts on a dpn and make 5-st I-cord: *K5, slide sts to front of dpn, bring yarn around back, pulling a bit. Repeat from *. The gap on the back will tighten after a few rows. Make the I-cord as long as you like.
K2tog across; cut yarn and pull through rem st. Weave in all ends neatly on WS.
Gently steam press to block.

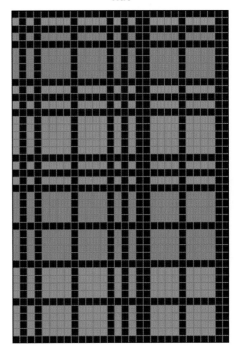

Hat

Tora

SOCKS, MITTENS, AND HAT

Size: Child's 3-4 years
Yarn: Shown here: Gjestal Silja sock yarn (80% wool / 20% nylon, 164 yd [150 m], 50 g)
Light Sport / Heavy Fingering
Yarn amounts (see individual patterns for yarn amounts):
Yellow 357
Brown 345
Gray-green 356
Needles: U.S. sizes 2.5 and 4 / 3 and 3.5 mm--set of 5 dpn for socks and mittens; short circular for hat
Gauge: 26 sts = 4 in / 10 cm
Adjust needle sizes to obtain correct gauge if necessary.

Socks

Yellow 50 g
Brown 50 g
Gray-green 50 g

With MC and smaller dpn, CO 48 sts. Join, being careful not to twist cast-on row. Work in k1tbl, p1 rib for approx. 1 ¼ in / 3 cm. On the last rnd, increase 6 sts evenly spaced around to 54 sts total. Change to larger needles if necessary for gauge for two-color stranded knitting. Follow the chart on p. 32, working in pattern until sock is 4 ¾ in / 12 cm long. Place 27 sts onto 1 dpn and work heel flap in pattern for approx. 2 in / 5 cm.

Use yellow to k2tog—a yellow stripe will run down the sock foot gusset. Work in pattern across ndls 2 and 3. At the beg of needle 4, sl 1 (yellow st), k1 with yellow and psso. Decrease the same way on every rnd until 54 sts remain. Continue in pattern until foot measures approx. 5 ¼ in / 13 cm or desired length to toe.

Toe

Work across ndl 1 until 3 sts remain. Sl 1 (yellow), k1 with yellow, psso. Work the next st in pattern (either yellow or brown). Knit the 2 first sts on the next needle tog with yellow and then complete ndl. Work across ndl 3 until 3 sts remain. Decrease as for ndl 1. Work decrease on ndl 4 as for ndl 2. Decrease the same way on every round until 6 sts remain. Cut yarn and pull through rem sts.

Make the other sock the same way. Weave in ends neatly on WS. Gently steam press socks to block.

Heel Gusset

Begin on RS. Mark the center st. Knit 4 sts past the center st, k2tog; turn. Sl 1 and tighten yarn a bit. Purl following pattern to 4 sts past center st, p2tog; turn. Sl 1, tighten yarn. Knit 5 sts past center st, k2tog; turn.

Continue the same way, working back and forth, until all the sts across have been worked. Divide sts over 2 dpn. Knit the sts from the center st to the end of needle (this is ndl 1). Pick up and knit approx. 12 sts along the side of the heel flap, using a crochet hook. Alternate colors as you pick up sts. Slip the first st (yellow) on ndl 2 over to ndl 1. Work in pattern across ndls 2 and 3, slipping the last st to ndl 4. Pick up and knit approx. 12 sts down heel flap with crochet hook and place them on ndl 4. Knit to end of rnd.
Knit to last 2 sts of ndl 1, making sure the color sequence is correct.

Mittens

Yellow 50 g
Brown 50 g (use leftover yarn from socks)
Gray-green 50 g

With brown and smaller dpn, CO 42 sts. Join, being careful not to twist cast-on row. Work in k1, p1 rib for approx. 2 ½ in / 6 cm. On the last rnd, increase 8 sts evenly spaced around to 50 sts total. Change to larger needles if necessary for gauge for two-color stranded knitting and work in pattern following the chart on p. 33.

Socks

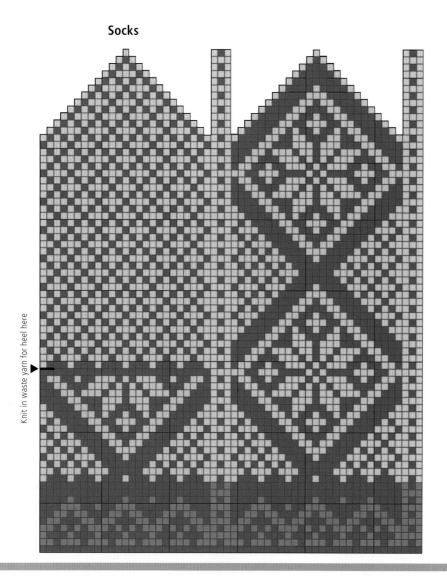

Knit in waste yarn for heel here

Hat

Where indicated on the chart, knit 11 sts with waste yarn, and continue in pattern, shaping top as indicated on the chart. Make the other mitten the same way, reversing placement of thumb so that you have a left and right mitten.

Thumb

Run a dpn through the 11 sts below the waste yarn and another dpn through the sts above the waste yarn. Pick up and knit 2 sts on each side and then work the thumb following the chart.

Weave in ends neatly on WS. Gently steam press socks to block.

Hat with three pompoms

Yellow 50 g
Brown 50 g (use leftover yarn from socks)
Gray-green 50 g

With MC and smaller size circular or dpn, CO 120 sts. Join, being careful not to twist cast-on row. Work 2 rnds k1tbl, p1 rib. Continue in rib pattern, working the k1tbl with yellow and the purl sts with gray-green for 5 rnds. If necessary for the gauge, change to larger needles.

Following the chart for the hat until you've worked a complete pattern or until hat is desired length. Knit 1 rnd with MC. Now shape the three-pointed top.

Thumb

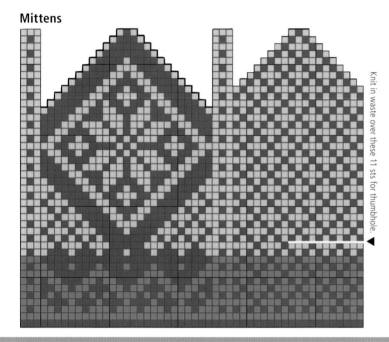

Mittens

Knit in waste over these 11 sts for thumbhole. ▲

Turn the work and begin on WS. Divide the sts evenly onto 4 dpn. Begin shaping where the yarn is. Place the 2 nearest ndls facing each other and use a third needle to knit. Knit first st from each needle tog, *Knit first st from each needle tog and pass the previous st over. Continue with three-needle bind-off (repeating from *) until you have bound-off 20 sts on each needle. Cut yarn, pull end through rem st and tighten. Now you have made a "peak."

Make sure there are 20 sts for the next peak. Begin bind off when there are 20 sts. Place the two needles with RS facing RS and bind off 20 sts (total of 40) as before and then you have peak #2. Cut yarn and pull end through rem st; tighten.

Divide the last 40 sts onto 2 dpn. Begin where the peak should be. Bind off 20 sts (40 total) as for previous two peaks and now you have peak #3.

Weave in all ends neatly on WS and gently steam press hat to block. Make sure there are no gaps at the top center of the hat. If there are, neatly sew them together. Securely sew a pompom at the center of the hat or on each peak.

Reidar

Mittens with a Clever Twist

100 g charcoal gray 227
50 g red 264
(You can use leftovers from the socks/mittens for the contrast colors.)
50 g yellow 218
50 g light green 213
50 g dark green 262
Needles: U.S. 4 and 6 / 3.5 and 4 mm--set of 5 dpn

The pattern chart is shown on page 36.

Size: Men's shoe size approx. U.S. 9 / European 43
Yarn: Gjestal Superwash Sport
(100% Wool, 109 yd [100 m], 50g)
Sport Weight
Yarn amounts for the entire set:
300 g charcoal gray 227
50 g yellow 218
50 g red 264
50 g light green 213
50 g dark green 262
Needles: U.S. sizes 4 and 6 / 3.5 and 4 mm--set of 5 dpn
for socks and mittens; short circular for hat
Gauge: 23 sts = 4 in / 10 cm
Adjust needle sizes to obtain correct gauge if necessary.

With smaller dpn and MC, CO 52 sts; divide the sts onto 4 dpn and join, being careful not to twist cast-on row. Work in k2, p2 rib for 2 ¾ in / 7 cm. Knit 1 rnd with charcoal gray, at the same time, increasing 12 sts evenly spaced around to a total of 64 sts. Change to larger dpn.

Work the small triangles pattern for the socks/hat. The main color is always charcoal gray and you can arrange the contrast colors depending on how much you have of each. Here's the color sequence we used for the model shown (see chart):

On the first 2 pattern repeats (6 rounds), the contrast color is yellow, the next three are light green before it changes to dark green. When you have worked 5 pattern repeats (or 15 rounds), knit the last 12 sts of ndl 1 with waste yarn. (For the left mitten, knit on the last 12 sts of ndl 2 with the waste yarn). Work in pattern for 15 more rounds. Cut yarn. Place the sts from ndls 3 and 4 on a holder. CO 32 sts with red. Work 10 rows stockinette back and forth. Divide the sts on ndl 2 (ndls 1 and 2 with the RS of the knitting facing out) and place the sts on the holder back onto ndls 3 ad 4. Knit 2 rnds with red over all the sts.

Fingers (with larger ndls)

When you are ready to knit the fingers, it will be useful to have 2-3 extra dpn on hand.

of middle finger. Divide these 21 sts onto 3 dpn and knit around until 2 fewer rnds than for middle finger. BO.

Little finger: Knit the last 7 sts on ndl 2 and the 7 sts remaining on ndl 3. Pick up 2 sts at base of ring finger. Divide these 16 sts onto 3 dpn and knit 14 rnds or to desired length. BO.

With charcoal and smaller ndls, CO 32 sts, knit 9 rows with k2, p2 rib. On the 10th row, work in stockinette on the RS. Divide sts onto 2 dpn (16 x 2) and pick up the sts on ndls 3 and 4 from the holders. Continue in pattern until the mitten measures 9 in / 23 cm or desired length. Shape top following the chart. (Use the same method of shaping as for the socks.)

Thumb

Pick up and knit the 12 sts above and below the waste yarn and remove the waste yarn. Pick up and knit 1 st at each side and work the thumb in pattern over these 26 sts until it is 2 ½-2 ¾ in / 6-7 cm long (see chart).

Make the other mitten the same way, reversing the placement of the thumb and fingers.

Index finger: Knit 9 sts on ndl 1, CO 2 sts and knit the last 9 sts on ndl 4. Slide the rest of the sts on ndl 4 to ndl 3 until later. Divide the 20 sts onto 3 dpn and knit 20 rnds or until desired finger length. BO.

Middle finger: Knit 8 sts on ndl 2. CO 3 new sts, knit the 8 sts nearest the index finger on ndl 3 and pick up and knit 2 sts at base of index finger. Divide these 21 sts onto 3 dpn. Knit about 25 rnds or to desired finger length. BO.

Ring finger: Work as for the middle finger but finish 2 rnds sooner. Knit 8, CO 2 sts, knit the 8 sts nearest the middle finger and pick up and knit 3 sts at base

Securely sew the finger piece to the top of the hand and then sew the rib panel at the sides.

Weave in all ends neatly on WS. Gently steam press mittens to block.

Ski Hat with a Neck to Fold Down

(…and if you don't want to fold it down, you can fold it up!)

100 g charcoal gray 227

50 g yellow 218 (you can use leftover yarn from the socks)

Experience has shown me if you fold the neck of this face mask up, the cap will look better with the large pattern on the back of the head so the opening for the face is more hidden.

With the smaller circular and MC, CO 132 sts; join, being careful not to twist cast-on row. Place a marker at beginning of rnd. Work in k2, p2 rib for 8 in / 20 cm. Next rnd: K2, p1. Knit the next 37 sts with a contrast color waste yarn. Slip these 37 sts back onto the left needle and continue with k2, p2 rib as set for another ¾ in / 2 cm. Knit 2 rnds and then change to larger circular.

Work in pattern following the chart for the hat.

After completing charted rows, knit 1 rnd and then work 2 rnds in k2, p2 rib. On the next rnd, work (k2, p2tog) around. Work 1 rnd (k2, p1 around). On the next rnd, work (k2tog, p1) around. On the last round, work (k2, k2tog) around. Cut yarn and pull through remaining sts; tighten.

Pick up 37 sts above and below the waste yarn. BO in k2, p2 rib around the opening. Cut yarn, weave in all ends neatly on WS and gently steam press hat to block (be especially careful on the ribbed edge – just hold the iron over the ribbing and apply steam without touching the knitting.)

Socks

150 g charcoal gray 227
50 g yellow 218
50 g red 264
50 g light green 213
50 g dark green 262

With smaller needles and charcoal, CO 72 sts, divide onto 4 dpn and join, being careful not to twist cast-on row. Work 9 rnds in k1tbl, p1 rib. Work charted panel 1. Knit the sock following the chart. Ndl 1 begins above the cast-on tail.

Heel Flap

Place the 31 sts at center back onto one dpn and work the heel flap back and forth for approx. 2 ½ in / 6 cm. The remaining sts can stay on their needles while you work the heel.

Hat

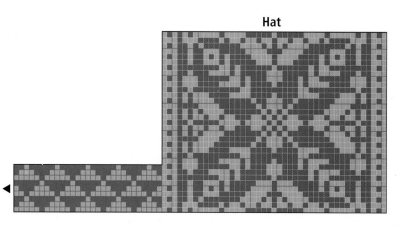

Continue in pattern until all the sts have been worked ◄

Mittens

The pattern is the same as the back of leg/sole pattern for the socks

Heel Gusset

Mark the center st with a locking ring marker. Work in pattern as set. Begin on RS and work until 5 sts past the center st. Slip the next st, knit the next st with charcoal gray and then psso (all the sts will be decreased with the charcoal). Turn. Slip the first st and tighten yarn. Work in pattern on WS until 5 sts past the center st. P2tog by inserting the needle in from the RS (= purl 2tog tbl)—don't forget to decrease with the charcoal! Continue working back and forth in pattern, decreasing as set until 13 sts remain. The decreases sts should now align smoothly one after the other as a charcoal gray line on each side.

The rnd now begins at the center st of heel. Knit the sts on the ndl. Pick up and knit 12-13 sts on the left side of the heel flap with a crochet hook. Alternate colors as you pick up sts. Slip the first 3 sts on ndl 2 to the needle you just used to pick up and knit for the heel flap. This is ndl 1. Work across ndls 2 and 3 in pattern. Slip the last 3 sts on ndl 3 to ndl 4. Pick up and knit 12-13 sts on the last needle with a crochet hook and then knit to center st of heel.

Foot gusset

Work across the sts on ndl 1, beginning at center st of heel until 4 sts remain. K2tog, using the pattern color (in this case, green). Work the last 2 sts on ndl 1 in pattern.

Work sock pattern over sts on ndls 2 and 3. Knit the first 2 sts on ndl 4 in pattern and then slip the 3rd st, k1 with green and psso. Continue in sole pattern. Decrease the same way on every round until 18 + 19 sts remain. Continue in charted pattern.

Toe Shaping

Move the last st on ndl 4 to ndl 1. Sl 1, k1 with green and psso. Knit across needle until 1 st remains. Place the first st on ndl 3 to ndl 2. K2tog with green.

Begin the next ndl with dark gray (or green if that works with the pattern), sl the green st, k1 with green, psso; knit rem sts on ndl.

Knit across next ndl until 3 sts remain. K2tog with green. Knit the last st with green or dark gray depending on pattern. Begin ndl 4 by slipping the green st, k1 with green and psso. Complete round. Continue decreasing the same way on every round until 6 sts remain. Cut yarn and pull through remaining sts; pull tightly. Weave in all ends neatly on WS. Gently steam press sock to block.

Make the other sock the same way.

Work the heel here ▶

▲ Center stitch   ▲ Center stitch

Ingunn

SOCKS WITH BOUCLÉ EDGING

Size: Women's medium shoe sizes approx. U.S. 7-8 /
European 37-38

Yarn: Gjestal Celine

(Bouclé, 97% Mohair / 3% Polyester, 38 yd [35 m], 50 g)

Super Bulky

Silja sock yarn (80% wool / 20% nylon, 164 yd [150 m], 50 g)

Light Sport / Heavy Fingering

Yarn amounts:

Celine red 709

Silja red 337

Silja blue 324

Tweed yarn (Orme) 330

Needles: U.S. sizes 2.5 and 4 / 3 and 3.5 mm--set of 5 dpn

Gauge: Silja 26 sts = 4 in / 10 cm

Celine 12 sts = 4 in / 10 cm on US 10.5

Adjust needle sizes to obtain correct gauge if necessary.

Socks

With 2 larger dpn held together (for a looser edge) and Celine, CO 30 sts; remove extra needle carefully. Knit 2 rows back and forth (as loosely as possible) with larger needles. Change to red Silja yarn and increase to 60 sts on the first row. Divide sts evenly onto 4 dpn. Work in pattern following the chart on page 41. When you come to the row for the heel, knit the heel with red and blue yarn as follows: Place 30 sts on one dpn and work back and forth with red and blue on alternate stitches. (On the model shown, the heel is knit with the smaller needles, but you can decide which needle size to use.) Work 18 rows with knit over knit and purl over purl and knit the final row.

Heel Gusset

Begin the gusset on the RS. Place a marker on the center st (15 sts on each side of center). K20 (following color sequence), k2tog (use the same color each time you knit 2 together); turn.

Sl 1 and tighten yarn slightly, p9 in color sequence, p2tog and turn. K9, k2tog (in color sequence) and turn. Continue the same way until you've worked across all the stitches.

Using a crochet hook, pick up and knit about 15 sts along the left side of the heel flap and place them on larger needles. Pick up red and blue sts alternately. Continue in pattern following the chart over the next 2 needles, working with larger dpn. Pick up and knit about 15 sts along the other side of the

heel flap. Divide the sts where the round changes at the center heel marker. Count out 15 sts on each side of the marked center st and work in the block pattern over these sts. The rest of the sts are worked with tweed orme yarn and decreased as follows: Work until 2 sts remain on ndl on left side (ndl 1), k2tog. Work across the 2 needles with the block pattern. On the last ndl, sl 1, k1, psso. Decrease the same way on every round until 60 sts remain.

Continue in block pattern over the entire foot until the foot is 8 in / 20 cm long or desired length.

Toe Shaping

Use only the red and blue yarn. Knit 1 round alternating red and blue sts. On the next rnd, begin shaping at each side. K1 blue, sl 1 red, k1 red, psso and complete sts on ndl. Knit until 3 sts remain on next ndl. K2 blue tog and k1 red. Work the last 2 ndls the same way. Decrease the same way until 8 sts remain. Cut yarn and pull through remaining sts; pull tightly. Make the other sock the same way.

Weave in all ends neatly on WS. Gently steam press socks to block.

Tips

I recommend that you twist the strands around each other when changing colors as you knit the blocks; otherwise, there will be long floats on the inside of the socks. You can also sew the strands with loose stitches on the WS when the socks are finished. If you don't follow either of these suggestions, the strands will shred and the socks will wear out quickly.

Socks

Heel

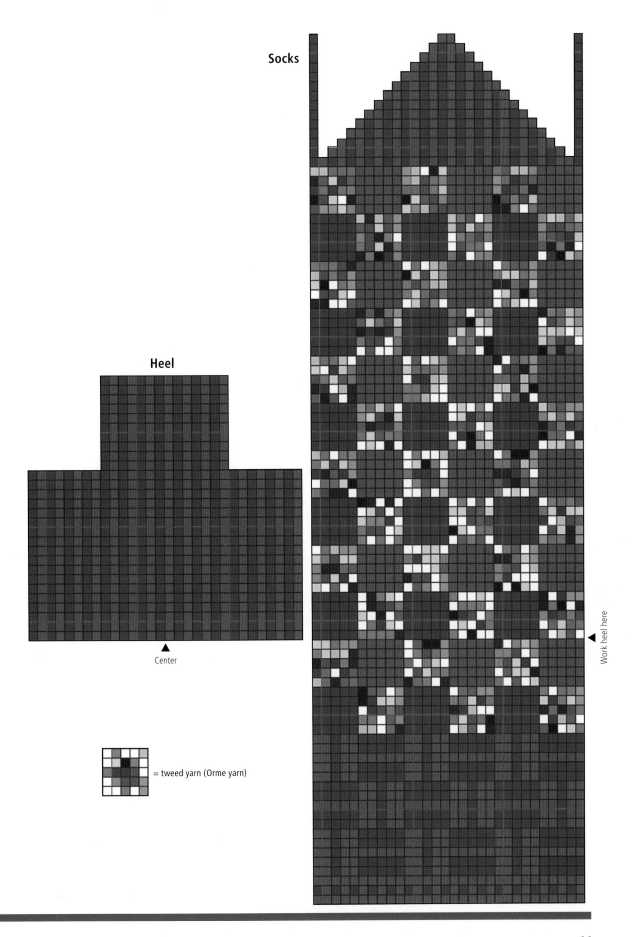

▲
Center

◄ Work heel here

= tweed yarn (Orme yarn)

Jorun

COTTON SOCKS AND NECK ROLL

Bed Socks

The pattern for the ribbing is a multiple of 3 sts.
Rnd 1: (P1, k2) around.
Rnd 2: (P1, knit the 2nd st from needle tip and then knit the 1st st) around. If it is easier for you, you can cross the cables as follows: sl 1 st to cable needle and hold in front; k1 and then k1 from cable needle.
Repeat these 2 rounds until the ribbing is as long as desired.

With smaller needles and MC (mint), CO 60 sts; divide sts onto 4 dpn and join, being careful not to twist cast-on row. Work in rib pattern described above until cuff measures 5 ¼ in / 13 cm or desired length. Now work the narrow red and yellow panel charted on the next page. Knit 1 rnd with MC and then 1 rnd blue. Begin the main pattern, beginning where the arrow indicates. After 3 rnds, knit in a strand of contrast color waste yarn over the sts on two needles (you'll knit the heel here later). Continue in pattern until the sock is desired length to toe. Shape the toe, decreasing as shown on the chart. Make another sock the same way.

Size: Women's shoe size approx. U.S. 9 / European 39
Yarn: Shown here: Gjestal Cotton Sport
(100% cotton, 110 yd [101 m], 50g)
Sport Weight
Yarn amounts for Socks:
100 g mint 312 (you can substitute blue 348 for the MC)
100 g blue 314
50 g red 322 (enough for the set)
50 g yellow 357 (enough for the set)
Yarn amounts for the pillow:
150 g MC and 150 g blue
Leftovers from socks for red and yellow
Needles: U.S. sizes 2.5 and 4 / 3 and 3.5 mm--set of 5 dpn for socks; short circulars for pillow
Gauge: 23 sts = 4 in / 10 cm
Adjust needle sizes to obtain correct gauge if necessary.

Heel

Pick up the stitches above and below the waste yarn at the heel; remove the waste yarn. Begin working on the underside of the heel and work following the chart. You'll soon notice that the heel is shaped just like the toe.

Weave in all ends neatly on WS. If you notice small holes at each side of the beginning of the heel, use the ends to close up the holes. Gently steam press socks to block.

Neck roll

The pillow is approx. 16 ¼ in / 41 cm long, with a circumference of 19 in / 48 cm. You can buy a pillow form for it at any fabric and furnishing shop.

End pieces

With smaller dpn and MC and CO 8 sts. Divide sts over 4 dpn and join to knit in the round.
Rnd 1: Knit.
Rnd 2: Increase (k1fb) in each st around = 16 sts.
Rnd 3: Knit.
Rnd 4: (K2, k1fb) around = 24 sts.
Rnd 5: Knit.
Rnd 6: (K3, k1fb) around = 32 sts.
Rnd 7: Knit.

Continue increasing on every other round, with 1 st more between increases until there are a total of 96 sts (the circumference should be 19 in / 48 cm). It is better to make the ends a little bit too small than too large. If you need to add more rounds, increase as set until the piece is the correct circumference. BO. Knit a second end the same way. Weave in all ends neatly on WS. Gently steam press to block.

Cylinder

With smaller circular and red, pick up and knit 96 sts around the edge of one end. On the first round, increase 4 sts evenly spaced

Pattern for the Socks, Heel and Toe Shaping

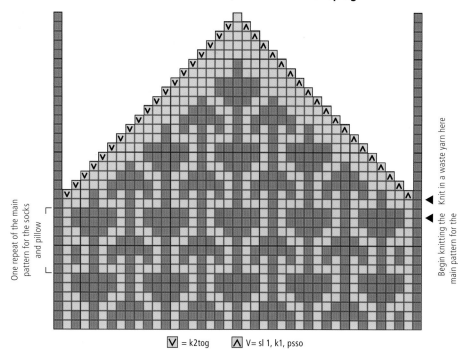

One repeat of the main pattern for the socks and pillow

Knit in a waste yarn here

Begin knitting the main pattern for the sock here

$\boxed{V}$ = k2tog $\boxed{\Lambda}$ V= sl 1, k1, psso

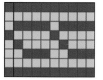

Narrow Panel for the Pillow Cover

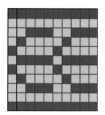

around. Knit a total of 14 rnds in stockinette over the 100 sts. With dpn, pick up 100 sts on the wrong side of the first round with red. Knit these sts together, one by one, with the live stitches on the circular to form the folded edge. If you prefer, you can sew the edges together once the cylinder is finished.

Change to larger circular, knit 1 round with red, increasing 5 sts evenly spaced around = 105 sts. Work the yellow and red pillow panel following the chart. Knit 1 rnd with MC and dec 1 st. Now continue in the main

pattern for about 11 ¾ in / 30 cm (the pattern repeat is marked on the chart for the socks). Decrease 1 st on the last round (with MC). Knit the narrow panel. Change to smaller circular or dpns.

Knit 14 rnd with red, decreasing 5 sts evenly spaced around on the first rnd = 100 sts. On Rnd 14, pick up stitches from the 2nd rnd with red and knit them together with the live sts for the folded edge. If you prefer, you can sew the edges together on the WS before you bind off for the completed pillow. Knit 1 more round and decrease 4 sts evenly spaced around = 96 sts. With dpn, pick up 48 sts. Knit the stitches together, one by one, as for the other end. BO remaining 48 sts.

Weave in all ends neatly on WS. Gently steam press pillow cover to block. Insert the pillow form and sew the opening closed.

Tips

If you found it too difficult to knit the second end piece with the pillow cover, knit it separately and sew it on when finishing. In any case, don't forget to leave an opening so you can insert the pillow form!

Socks with Doubled Cuff

150 g gray 205
100 g dark rose 293
50 g purple 292

With gray and smaller dpn, CO 60 sts; divide sts evenly over 4 dpn and join, being careful not to twist cast-on row. Work 3 rnds k1, p1 rib. Knit 1 rnd before beginning the pattern for the doubled cuff. After completing charted cuff pattern, knit 2 rnds with gray. Now work eyelet row for foldline: (K2tog, yo) around. Next, knit 5 rnds in stockinette. Turn work inside out. Knit 5 rnds stockinette and, on the last rnd, increase 2 sts evenly spaced around = 62 sts total. Begin charted pattern, working the two half "roses" (see page 48).

Heel Flap

Work back and forth in pattern over the 31 sts at center back for approx. 2 ½ in / 6 cm. Use rose as the pattern color for the star panel as shown on the chart. When you begin shaping the heel gusset, you need to be careful to keep the pattern centered over the center stitch.

Heel Gusset

Begin on RS. Mark the center st. Work in pattern until 5 sts past the center st. Sl 1, k1 gray (all of the decreases should be worked with gray to create a smooth line of gray stitch-es). Turn. Sl 1, tighten yarn, and purl in pattern until 5 sts past center st, p2tog with gray. Continue decreasing the same way until you've worked all the sts across = 13 sts remain.
The round and ndl 1 now begin at the

Kari

SOCKS, HEADBAND, AND HALF-GLOVES

Size: Women's shoe size approx. US 9 / European 39
Yarn: Shown here: Gjestal Superwash Sport
(100% wool, 109 yd [100 m], 50g)
Sport Weight
Yarn amounts for Set:
200 g gray 205
50 g purple 292
100 g dark rose 293
Needles: U.S. sizes 2.5 and 4-6 / 3 and 3.5-4 mm--set of
5 dpn for socks and half-gloves + 3 extra dpn for glove
fingers; short circulars for headband
Gauge: 23 sts = 4 in / 10 cm
Adjust needle sizes to obtain correct gauge if necessary.

center st. Knit the rest of the sts on ndl 1. Using crochet hook, pick up about 10 sts along the left edge of the heel flap, alternating gray and rose. Slip the first rose st of ndl 2 onto ndl 1. Work across ndls 2 and 3, following charted pattern. Slip the last rose st on ndl 3 to ndl 4. Pick up approx. 10 sts along the right edge of heel flap using the crochet hook and then knit to the center heel st.

Foot Gusset

Knit across ndl 1 (don't forget to work in the star pattern!) until 2 sts remain; k2tog with rose. On ndl 2, sl 1 (rose), k1 rose and psso. Continue in pattern until 2 sts rem on ndl 3. Decrease as for ndl 1. Decrease on ndl 4 as for ndl 2. Decrease the same way on every round until 64 sts remain and the charted patterns align. Work the foot following the chart.

Toe Shaping

Shape the toe as you did the foot gusset until 6 sts remain. Cut yarn and pull through remaining sts; pull tightly. Weave in all ends neatly on WS. Gently steam press sock to block. Make the other sock the same way.

Half-Gloves

100 g gray 205
50 g dark rose 293
50 g purple 292
(You can use the leftover rose and purple from the socks)

Note: If necessary for gauge, use larger needles for the two-color stranded knitting and smaller needles for the rib and single color fingers.

With smaller dpn and gray, CO 48 sts; divide sts evenly over 4 dpn

Socks

▶ Knit heel here

Half-Gloves

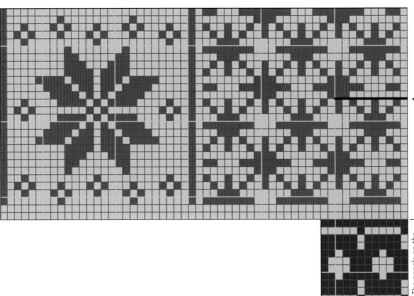

Knit these 10 sts with waste yarn for thumbhole ▶

The panels on the half-gloves and the socks are worked in the same pattern

48

Middle Finger

With gray, pick up and knit 4 sts at base of ring finger + remaining sts = 22 sts. Divide onto 3 dpn and knit around until finger is desired length. BO.

Thumb

Place the 10 sts below and above the waste yarn each onto a separate needle and then remove waste yarn. With rose, pick up and knit 1 st at each side = 22 sts. Divide over 3 dpn and knit around to desired length. BO.

Cut yarn and weave in all ends neatly on WS. Gently steam press glove to block.
Make the other glove the same way, reversing placement of thumbhole and fingers.

and join, being careful not to twist cast-on row. Work 3 rnds k1tbl, p1 rib. Now work the narrow purple panel. Next, knit 1 rnd gray, increasing 8 sts evenly spaced around to 56 sts total. Work the hand pattern. At the dark line on the chart, knit the 10 sts with a contrast color waste yarn. Complete charted rows of pattern. On the last round (gray) you can bind the rose sts off loosely to avoid carrying the rose around.

Little Finger

Place the last 7 sts on ndl 2 and the first 7 sts of ndl 3 onto 2 new needles. CO 4 sts between the two needles (between the fingers), and divide the 18 sts onto 3 dpn. Knit around with rose until the finger is desired length. BO knitwise for a smooth edge.
Continue with gray over the remaining sts. When you come to the space between the little finger and the ring finger, pick up and knit 4 sts in the cast-on sts = 46 sts. Knit 3 rounds over all the sts.

Index Finger

With gray, pick up the last 8 sts on ndl 4 and the first 8 sts of ndl 1. Cast on 4 sts between the fingers. Divide the 20 sts onto 3 dpn and knit around until finger is desired length. BO.
Knit 1 rnd with remaining sts. When you come to the space between the index and middle fingers, pick up and knit 4 sts in the cast-on sts = 34 sts. These will be divided for the middle and ring fingers.

Ring Finger

Begin the round at the center of the index finger with gray. Two of the sts you picked up are the beginning of rnd. Continue until you have 9 sts on the needle. CO 4 sts at the base of the middle finger and knit them as well as the 7 sts nearest the index finger (the 2 sts you picked up are the last sts). You should now have 20 sts to divide over 3 dpn. Knit around until finger is desired length and then BO.

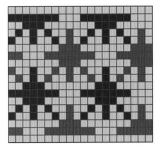

Headband

Use yarns leftover from socks and gloves. The pattern is a multiple of 21 sts.

With gray and short circular U.S. 2.5 or 4 / 3 or 3.5 mm, CO 126 sts; join, being careful not to twist cast-on row. Place marker for beginning of round. Knit 9 rnds in stockinette. Now work eyelet row for foldline: (K2tog, yo) around. Knit 1 rnd. Now work in pattern following the chart. After completing charted rows, work another eyelet round; knit 9 rnds (with rose if desired), and then BO. Gently steam press headband before seaming the cast-on and bound-off edges.

Headband

Andris

SOCKS AND HAT

Size: Men's shoe sizes approx. U.S. 10 ½-11 ½ /
European 44-45
Yarn: Shown here: Gjestal Vestland yarn
(100% wool, 109 yd [100 m], 50g)
4-ply Worsted
Yarn amounts for Socks:
150 g blue 232, 100 g turquoise 211
Yarn amounts for Hat:
100 g blue 232, 100 g turquoise 211
Needles: U.S. sizes 2.5 and 4 / 3 and 3.5mm--set of
5 dpn for socks; short circulars for hat
Gauge: 26 sts = 4 in / 10 cm
Adjust needle sizes to obtain correct gauge if necessary.

Socks

With smaller dpn and MC, CO 60 sts; divide sts onto 4 dpn and join, being careful not to twist cast-on row. Work in k1tbl, p1 rib for 1 ¼ in / 3 cm. Knit 1 rnd, increasing 12 sts evenly spaced around to 72 sts. Now knit the narrow panel. Increase 1 st more = 73 sts and then continue the charted pattern on the next page. Work in pattern for 6 ¼ in / 16 cm.

Heel

Begin the heel over the 2 back needles (that is 37 sts) and move the sts onto one dpn. Work back and forth in pattern until the heel flap is 2 ½ in / 6 cm long. Mark the center st. Begin decreasing on RS. Knit until 5 sts past the center st. Ssk, k1 and turn.

Sl 1, tightening yarn slightly. Purl in pattern until 5 sts past the center st, p2tog, p1 and turn.

Sl 1, tightening yarn slightly. K12, ssk, k1 and turn.

Sl 1, tightening yarn slightly, p13, p2tog, p1, turn.

Continue decreasing the same way until all the sts have been worked.

Foot gussets

Ndl 1 begins at the center heel st. Pick up approx. 12 sts along the edge of the heel flap with a crochet hook. Alternate the colors when picking up stitches, making sure that the last st is green. Knit across ndls 2 and 3 in pattern. On ndl 4, pick up and knit approx. 12 sts along edge of heel flap, using crochet hook (the first st

should be turquoise); knit to end of ndl. Knit across ndl 1 until 2 sts remain and then k2tog with turquoise. Knit across ndls 2 and 3. Begin ndl 4 with sl 1 (green), k1 with turquoise, psso; complete rnd. Decrease the same way on every round until 73 sts remain. Continue foot in pattern until it is desired length (on sock shown here, the foot is 6 ¾ in / 17 cm as measured from the heel gusset.

Toe Shaping

Knit across ndl 1 until 2 sts remain, k2tog with turquoise.

Begin the next needle with blue or turquoise depending on pattern, sl 1 turquoise, k1 turquoise and psso. Complete needle. Work across ndl 3 until 3 sts remain k2tog with turquoise, k1 with blue or turquoise in color sequence. Begin ndl 4 with sl 1 turquoise, k1 with turquoise, psso. Complete round.

Decrease the same way on every round until 6 sts remain. Cut yarn and pull through remaining sts; pull end tight. Weave in all ends neatly on WS. Gently steam press sock to block.

Make the other sock the same way.

Hat

With MC and smaller circular, CO 120 sts; join, being careful not to twist cast-on row. Place marker at beginning of round. Work in k1tbl, p1 rib for about 4 in / 10 cm. Knit 1 rnd, increasing 19 sts evenly spaced around to 139 sts. Work in pattern following the hat chart. Change to larger circular if necessary for gauge. After completing charted rows, continue in MC until hat measures approx. 9 ¾ in / 25 cm (try it on to be sure it fits!). K2tog around. Knit 1 rnd. K2tog around. Cut yarn and pull end through remaining sts; tighten end. Cut yarn and pull through remaining sts; pull tightly. Weave in all ends neatly on WS. Gently steam press hat to block. If you like, make a tassel or pompom to sew securely to the top.

Socks

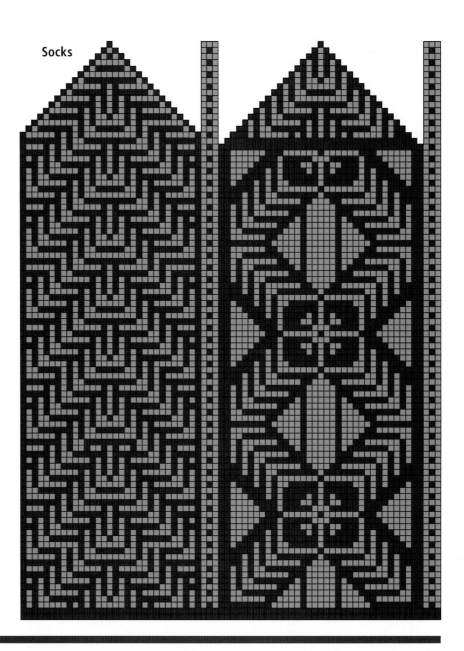

Panel for the Socks

Hat

*If you want a wider circumference for the hat, you can increase by knitting the sts marked with
* 2 times. The hat will then have 2 stripes at each side with a blue stitch in between.

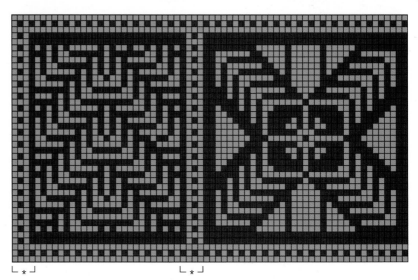

Toril

COTTON SOCKS WITH FOLDED CUFF

Size: Women's shoe sizes approx. U.S. 7-8 / European 37-38

Yarn: Shown here: Gjestal Cotton Sport
(100% cotton, 110 yd [101 m], 50g)
Sport Weight

Yarn amounts for Socks:
100 g MC light blue 348
100 g deep pink 315
50 g blue 314 (use leftovers!)
50 g blue 344 (use leftovers!)

Needles: U.S. sizes 4 and 6 / 3.5 and 4 mm--set of 5 dpn and short circulars

Gauge: 23 sts = 4 in / 10 cm

Adjust needle sizes to obtain correct gauge if necessary.

Socks

The pattern on the folded cuff is a multiple of 14 and the pattern on the socks is 8 + 1 sts.

With smaller dpn and blue 314, CO 56 sts; divide sts onto 4 dpn and join, being careful not to twist cast-on row. Work 2 rnds k1tbl, p1 rib. On the following 4 rnds, work the twisted knit with blue 344 which is the main color for the folded cuff. Work the cuff pattern following the chart. Knit 2 rnds with blue 314. Purl 1 rnd and then knit 3 rnds.

Change to color 348 which is now the MC for the sock and knit 3 rnds in stockinette.

Turn the sock inside out. The folded cuff will face correctly once you fold it down. Increase 1 st at beginning of next round and knit 6 rnds total before beginning the main pattern. Work in pattern until the sock measures 6 ¾ in / 17 cm from the foldline.

Heel Flap

Place 21 sts onto one dpn and knit 1 st with blue 344, 1 st blue 348 back and forth until heel flap is approx. 2 in / 5 cm long. Begin decreasing on the RS. K14, sl 1, k1 in the same color as the slipped st, psso. There should now be 6 sts remaining at end of ndl; turn. Sl 1 and tighten yarn slightly, p7 (in color sequence), p2tog—6 sts remain on ndl. Turn. Continue, decreasing the same way until all the sts have been worked and there are 9 center sts. Divide these sts onto 2 ndls (4 + 5 sts). Cut the dark blue yarn. Finish ndl and pick

up and knit approx. 15 sts using a crochet hook along the edge of the heel flap = 20 sts on ndl 1. Work in pattern over the next two ndls (ndls 2 and 3). Using crochet hook, pick up and knit approx. 15 sts along other side of heel flap and place them on ndl 4 along with the 4 sts from heel (19 sts on ndl 4). Cut yarn and reattach to begin rnd where the pattern begins on ndl 2. Continue in pattern on all 4 ndls. Eliminate the extra sts for gusset as follows: Work across ndls 2 and 3. On ndl 4, sl 1, knit the next st with rose and psso. When 2 sts remain on ndl 1, k2tog with rose. Decrease the same way on every round until 57 sts remain.

Continue in leg/foot pattern all around the foot until foot measures 8 in / 20 cm or desired length. Decrease the last st on the round so that the total is divisible by 2.

Toe shaping

Alternate rounds of blue 348 and blue 344 (see chart). Knit 1 rnd. On the next rnd, begin shaping: on ndl 2:, k1, sl 1, k1, psso; knit to end of needle. On ndl 3, knit until 3 sts remain, k2tog, k1. Work ndl 4 as for ndl 2 and ndl 1 as for ndl 3. When 8 sts remain, cut yarn and pull through remaining sts; pull tight.

Make the other sock the same way.

Weave in all ends neatly on WS. Gently steam press sock to block. Fold the cuffs down.

Toe **Heel** **Cuffs** **Leg/Foot Pattern for Socks**

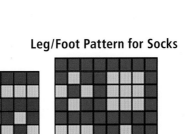

Sylvia

SOCKS, HEADBAND, AND HALF-MITTENS

Size: Women's shoe size approx. U.S. 8 / European 38
Yarn: Shown here: Gjestal Vestland yarn
(100% wool, 109 yd [100 m], 50g)
4-ply Worsted
Yarn amounts for Socks:
200 g blue 232
100 g blue 207
Needles: U.S. sizes 4 and 6 / 3.5 and 4 mm--set of 5 dpn
for socks and gloves; short circular for headband
Gauge: 23 sts = 4 in / 10 cm
Adjust needle sizes to obtain correct gauge if necessary.
The pattern for Jenny's socks and hat with earflaps can
be found on pages 59-60.

Socks

With smaller dpn and light blue, CO 48 sts; divide sts onto 4 dpn and join, being careful not to twist cast-on row. Work 9 rnds k2, p2 rib. Change to larger dpn and block pattern (see chart on next page). Next, work stripe pattern, increasing 5 sts evenly spaced around to 53 sts on the last round.

Heel Flap

Work back and forth in block pattern over 26 sts until there are 6 rows of blocks.

Heel Gusset

Place a marker between sts 13 and 14. Begin decreasing on the RS. Knit until 4 sts past the center st. K2tog (always decrease with the MC); turn. Sl 1, purl across in pattern until 4 sts past center st. P2tog with MC. Turn and knit until you come to the previous st you knit together. Knit that st tog with the next st. Turn and purl to the st previously decreased; purl that st together with the next st. Continue decreasing the same way until you've worked all the sts = 11 sts remain. End on RS and work to end of ndl.

With a crochet hook, pick up and knit 10-12 sts along the left side of the heel flap. Alternate colors when picking up sts. Knit across ndls 2 and 3 in pattern. Pick up the same number of sts along right side of heel flap as for left side. Continue in pattern decreasing as follows: Knit from the center heel st until 2 sts remain on ndl 1 and k2tog with MC. Work across ndls 2-3 in pattern. Begin last ndl with sl 1, k1 with MC, psso, knit to end of ndl. Decrease the same way on every round until 53 sts remain. Continue, following the chart.

Toe Shaping

Knit from the center heel marker until 2 sts remain on ndl 1 and k2tog with dark blue. Work all of the decreases with dark blue. On the next ndl, sl 1, k1 with dark blue, psso, knit rem sts on ndl 2. Knit across ndl 3 until 2 sts remain and end k2tog. On ndl 4, begin with sl 1, k1, psso. Decrease the same way on every round until 7 sts remain. Cut yarn and pull through remaining sts; pull tightly. Weave in all ends neatly on WS. Gently steam press sock to block.
Make the other sock the same way.

Half-Mittens

With dark blue and smaller dpn, CO 40 sts. Knit 3 rows back and forth. Join to work in the round, divide sts over 4 dpn, and work 9 rnds k2, p2 rib. On the last rnd, increase 8 sts evenly spaced around to 48 sts (12 sts per dpn). Change to larger dpn and work in block pattern. Begin shaping the thumb gusset on the stripe pattern: On the last rnd of the first stripe, increase 1 st at the beginning and increase 1 st at the end the rnd. Increase the same way on every 3rd rnd of the next 4 stripes until there are 20 sts for thumb. Place the 20 sts on a holder.

Now continue in pattern over the remaining 48 sts. Work 2 stripes more (or as many as you like), ending with garter st worked back and forth (4 rows)*. BO.
Pick up the 20 sts on holder for thumb and divide over 3 dpn. Work 2 stripes, knit 4 rows back and forth and then BO (as for hand).

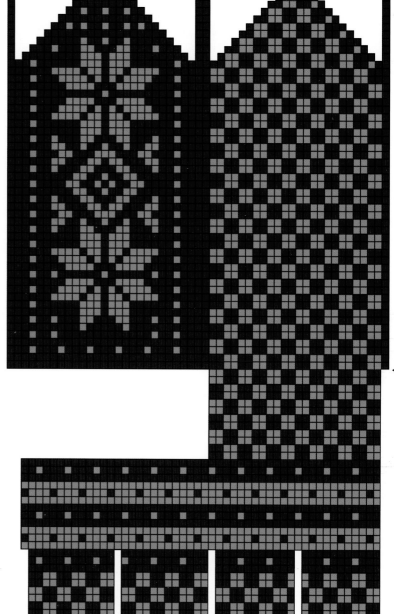

Socks

Knit heel here

* If you want to continue in the round for the garter stitch, alternate knit and purl rounds. Make one more glove the same way. Weave in all ends neatly on WS. Gently steam press to block.

Headband

With smaller short circular and dark blue, CO 128 sts, join, being careful not to twist cast-on row. Place marker for beginning of round. Knit 8 rnds in stockinette with dark blue. Next, make an eyelet row for the fold: (K2tog, yo) around. Knit the next rnd. Now work in pattern following the chart. Make another eyelet round and then knit 8 rnds with dark blue. BO. Gently steam press the headband, folding at each eyelet row. Seam the bound-off and cast-on rows.

Heel Gusset

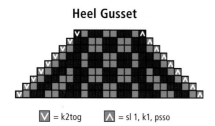

$\boxed{\text{V}}$ = k2tog	$\boxed{\wedge}$ = sl 1, k1, psso

Half-Mittens

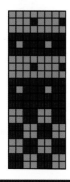

Headband

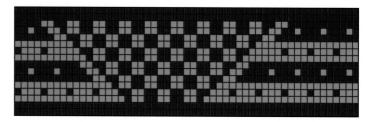

Socks

With smaller dpn and dark blue, CO 40 sts; divide sts evenly over 4 dpn. Join, being careful not to twist cast-on row. Work 7 rnds k1tbl, p1 rib. On the last rnd, increase 8 sts evenly spaced around to 48 sts. Change to larger dpn if necessary to obtain gauge. Work in pattern following the chart until sock measures 4 in / 10 cm.

Jenny

SOCKS AND HAT WITH EARFLAPS

Size: 3-4 years
Yarn: Gjestal Vestland yarn (100% wool, 109 yd [100 m], 50g)
4-ply Worsted
Yarn amounts for the Set:
100 g blue 232
100 g blue 207
Needles: U.S. 4 and 6 / 3.5 and 4 mm--set of 5 dpn
Gauge: 23 sts = 4 in / 10 cm
Adjust needle sizes to obtain correct gauge if necessary.

Heel Flap

Place the 23 sts in the small background pattern onto one dpn and work back and forth in pattern for approx. 1 ½ in / 4 cm. Make sure that the pattern aligns.

Heel Gusset

Begin on RS. Mark the center st. Knit until 3 sts past the center st, k2tog; turn.

Sl 1 purlwise, tightening yarn slightly. Purl until 3 sts past the center st, p2tog; turn.

Sl 1 purlwise, tightening yarn slightly, knit until 4 sts past the center st, k2tog; turn.

Continue decreasing the same way until you've worked across all the sts. Divide the heel sts onto 2 dpn. The round now begins at the center st. Knit to the end of the heel sts and then, with the crochet hook, pick up and knit 8-10 sts along the edge of the heel

Foot Gusset

Knit across ndl 1 until 2 sts rem; end k2tog. Knit across ndls 2 and 3. Begin ndl 4 with sl 1, k1 with light blue, psso and knit to end of ndl. Decrease the same way on every round until 48 sts rem.

flap. Knit in pattern across ndls 2 and 3. Use crochet hook to pick up and knit 8-10 sts on the other side of the heel; complete round.

Heel Shaping

Socks

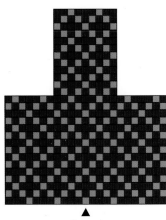

▲
Center st

Hat

Continue the foot in pattern until it is approx. 5 ¼ in / 13 cm long or desired length.

Toe Shaping

Knit across ndl 1 until 3 sts rem; sl 1, k1 with light blue, psso and then knit last st. K2tog at beginning of ndl 2 and work across ndl. Knit across ndl 3 until 3 sts rem and then dec as for ndl 1. Work ndl 4 as for ndl 2. Decrease the same way on every round until 6 sts rem. Cut yarn and pull through remaining sts; pull tight.

Make the other sock the same way. Weave in all ends neatly on WS. Gently steam press sock to block.

*If you want to increase the size of the hat, increase 4 to 8 sts at the two places marked on the pattern chart.

Hat

With dark blue yarn and larger needles, CO 114 (124) sts; join, being careful not to twist cast-on row. Place marker for beginning of rnd. Knit 1 rnd. Begin charted pattern behind the right ear. Work in pattern until the hat measures approx. 7 ½ in / 19 cm. Knit 2 rnds of (k2, k2tog) around. Cut yarn and pull through rem sts; pull end to tighten.

Earflaps

With dark blue and larger ndls, pick up and knit 19 sts below the star panel. CO 19 more sts and then divide these 38 sts onto 4 dpn. Work around following the chart for the earflaps. Make another earflap the same way on the opposite side of the hat.

Facing

With smaller needles and light blue, pick up and knit 19 sts on the inside edge of the right earflap: pick up sts along the front edge, along the left ear flap and along the small pattern. There should now be 114 (124) sts total. Knit 10 rnds in stockinette (the right side of the facing should be the same as for RS of hat). Bind off.

Earflaps

Cut yarn and weave in all ends neatly on WS. Gently steam press hat to block. Turn facing in along the dark blue edge and sew it to the inside of the hat. Make tassels for the top by twisting together strands of both colors. If desired, you can also twist cords to sew onto the ends of the earflaps so the hat can be tied under the chin.

Peder

SOCKS

Size: 3-4 years
The socks for Peder are the same as the pair for Jenny, but with red and green. See the pattern instructions and charts on pages 59-60.

Håvard

SOCKS

Size: Men's shoe size approx. U.S. 9 / European 43
Yarn: Shown here: Gjestal Superwash Sport
(100% Superwash wool, 109 yd [100 m], 50g)
Sport Weight
Yarn Amounts:
150 g yellow 218
100 g red 209
100 g brown 245
50 g turquoise 211
Needles: U.S. sizes 4 and 6 / 3.5 and 4 mm--set of 5 dpn
Gauge: 26 sts = 4 in / 10 cm
Adjust needle sizes to obtain correct gauge if necessary.

The pattern is a multiple of 22 sts.

Socks

◄ Knit heel here

Heel

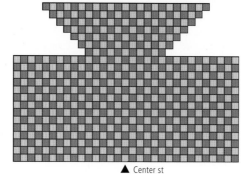

▲ Center st

Socks using leftover yarns

Håvard's socks are knit with leftover yarns with yellow as the main color throughout. Of course, you can knit the socks with whatever yarn you like that has the same gauge. I used Gjestal Superwash Soft for this model.

With smaller dpn and red, CO 66 sts; divide sts onto 4 dpn. Join, being careful not to twist cast-on row. Work 8 rnds k1tbl, p1 rib. Work in pattern following the chart. When leg is 5 ½ in / 14 cm long, knit the heel. Because this was one of the first color pattern socks that I knitted, the heel doesn't have any shaping. You can make the heel another way if you like (see Heel Gusset, page 6). I worked the heel as follows:
Knit the heel flap back and forth over the 31 sts at center back for approx. 2 ¼ in / 5.5 cm. Mark the center st. To add some length to the heel, beginning on RS, knit 5 sts past the center st; turn. Sl 1, tightening yarn slightly. P11 and turn. K13; turn; p14; turn, etc. Work back and forth the same way until you've worked over all the sts.
The round now begins at the center st on ndl 1. Work across ndl 1 and then, using a crochet hook, pick up and knit about 13 sts along

the edge of the heel flap. Alternate colors when picking up sts; the last st should be brown. Work the star pattern across ndls 2 and 3. Pick up and knit about 13 sts along the other side of the heel flap. The first st should be brown.

Foot Gussets
Work across ndl 1 until 2 sts remain, k2tog with brown. Work in pattern across ndls 2 and 3. Begin ndl 4 with sl 1 (brown), k1 with brown, psso; complete rnd.
Decrease the same way on every round until 66 sts rem.
Continue knitting the foot until the star pattern is complete or the foot is desired length.

Toe Shaping
Knit across ndl 1 until 3 sts remain; k2tog with yellow. Knit the last st with brown or yellow depending on the pattern. Begin ndl 2 with sl 1, k1 with yellow, psso, work to end of ndl. Work ndl 3 as for ndl 1 and ndl 4 as for ndl 2. Decrease the same way on every round until 4 sts remain.
Cut yarn and pull through remaining sts; pull tightly. Weave in all ends neatly on WS. Gently steam press sock to block.
Make the other sock the same way.

Yarn Information

For more information on selecting or substituting yarn contact your local yarn shop or an online store; they are familiar with all types of yarns and would be happy to help you. Additionally, the online knitting community at Ravelry.com has forums where you can post questions about specific yarns. Yarns come and go so quickly and there are so many beautiful yarns available; we have suggested substitutions for each of the yarns used in this book.

Gjestal Baby 8/4 Cotton
100% Mercerized Cotton
187 yd (171 m), 50 g
4-ply Fingering
28 sts = 4 in (10 cm)
Substitution-
Rowan Classic Siena
100% Mercerized Cotton
153 yd (140 m), 50 g
Fingering
28 sts = 4 in (10 cm)

Gjestal Silja Wool / Nylon
80% Wool, 20% Nylon
164 yd (150 m), 50 g
Light Sport or Heavy Fingering
26 sts = 4 in (10 cm)
Substitution-
Cascade Yarns 220 Sport
100% Peruvian Highland Wool
164 yd (150 m), 50 g
DK
5.5-6 sts = 1 in on US 5-6
or
Lorna's Laces Shepherd Sport
100% Superwash Merino Wool
200 yd (183 m), 70 g
Sport Weight
6 sts = 1 in on US 4

Gjestal Vestland
100% Wool
109 yd (100 m), 50 g
4-ply Worsted,
23-24 sts = 4 in (10 cm)
Substitution-
Lorna's Laces Shepherd Sport
100% Superwash Merino Wool
200 yd (183 m), 70 g
Sport Weight
6 sts = 1 in on US 4

Gjestal Superwash Sport
100% wool
109 yd (100 m), 50 g
Sport Weight
23 sts = 4 in (10 cm)
Substitution-
Lorna's Laces Shepherd Sport
100% Superwash Merino Wool
200 yd (183 m), 70 g
Sport Weight
6 sts = 1 in on US 4

Gjestal Celine
Bouclé
97% Mohair, 3% Polyester
38 yd (35 m), 50 g
Super Bulky
12 sts = 4 in (10 cm) on US 10.5
Substitution-
Garnstudio DROPS Puddel
94% Mohair, 6% Polyester
54 yd (49 m), 50 g
Bulky
10 sts = 4 in on 11 US

Gjestal Cotton Sport
100% cotton
110 yd (101 m), 50 g
Sport Weight
22-23 sts = 4 in (10 cm)
Substitution-
Sublime Egyptian Cotton DK
100% Cotton
115 yd (105 m), 50 g
DK
5.5 sts = 1 in on US 6
or
SMC Cotton Time
100% Cotton
96 yd (88 m), 50 g
DK
5.25 sts = 1 in on US 4-7

Gjestal website-
www.gjestal.no

Garnstudio website-
www.garnstudio.com

Webs – America's Yarn Store
75 Service Center Road
Northampton, MA 01060
800-367-9327
www.yarn.com
customerservice@yarn.com